First World War
and Army of Occupation
War Diary
France, Belgium and Germany

39 DIVISION
Composite Brigade
3 Composite Battalion
1 April 1918 - 30 April 1918

WO95/2587/3

The Naval & Military Press Ltd
www.nmarchive.com
Published in association with The National Archives

Published by

The Naval & Military Press Ltd

Unit 10 Ridgewood Industrial Park,

Uckfield, East Sussex,

TN22 5QE England

Tel: +44 (0) 1825 749494

www.naval-military-press.com

www.nmarchive.com

This diary has been reprinted in facsimile from the original. Any imperfections are inevitably reproduced and the quality may fall short of modern type and cartographic standards.

© **Crown Copyright**
Images reproduced by permission of The National Archives, London, England, 2015.

Contents

Document type	Place/Title	Date From	Date To
Heading	WO95/2587/3		
Heading	No. 3 Composite Bn Composite Bde. Apr 1918		
War Diary		11/04/1918	30/04/1918
War Diary	Appendix "A"	28/04/1918	28/04/1918
Heading	1/16th Battalion Notts & Derby Regiment April 1918		
War Diary	Longues	01/04/1918	01/04/1918
War Diary	Bovelles	02/04/1918	03/04/1918
War Diary	Metigny	04/04/1918	04/04/1918
War Diary	Forceville	05/04/1918	06/04/1918
War Diary	Flequires	07/04/1918	09/04/1918
War Diary	Moulle	10/04/1918	10/04/1918
War Diary	Listergauz	11/04/1918	14/04/1918
War Diary	Ridge Wood Camp	15/04/1918	15/04/1918
War Diary	Wytchaete	16/04/1918	16/04/1918
War Diary	Scottish Wood Camp	18/04/1918	18/04/1918
War Diary	English Wood Camp	19/04/1918	19/04/1918
War Diary	Awapuni Camp	20/04/1918	25/04/1918
War Diary	Vierstraat	25/04/1918	25/04/1918
War Diary	Voormezeele	26/04/1918	26/04/1918
War Diary	Dominion Camp	27/04/1918	30/04/1918

was 2/25/87 #3

39TH DIVISION
117TH INFY BDE

NO.3 COMPOSITE BN
COMPOSITE BDE.
APR 1918

NO. 3 COMPOSITE BATTALION, 39TH DIVISIONAL COMPOSITE BRIGADE.

WAR DIARY
or
INTELLIGENCE SUMMARY.
(Erase heading not required.)

Army Form C. 2118.

Place	Date	Hour	Summary of Events and Information	Remarks and references to Appendices
	1918		Period April 11th to 30th incl.	
	11th		Reference Maps :- Hazebrouck 5a - Sheet 27 Belgium and France -Sheet 28 Belgium & France.	
			Lieut. Colonel The Hon. E.COKE, D.S.O., M.C., (Commanding Officer, 16th Bn. The Rifle Brigade) Captain & Adjutant. G.V.TAYLOR M.C., 8 Officers and two Companies 16th Bn. Sherwood Foresters, 6 Officers and 12 Companies 17th Bn. King's Royal Rifle Corps, and 2 Company 16th Bn. The Rifle Brigade formed No.3 Battalion, 39th Division Composite Brigade. This Composite Battalion proceeded by march route to ST.OMER and entrained at 8 a.m. detraining at VIAMERTINGHE at 12 noon and marched to billets in ALBERTA CAMP, near RENINGHELST. The Battalion was accompanied by Transport of 16th Bn. Sherwood Foresters and Quartermaster's Stores of 17th Bn. King's Royal Rifle Corps. Remainder of details of units remained in rest billets under orders of 117th Infantry Brigade.	
	12th		Composite Battalion moved by Light Railway from ZEVECOTEN(28.G.35.d.) to JELLICOE Siding (28.H.36.c.) and billeted in FORESTER CAMP (28.H.30.d.). Battalion became under orders of 21st Division.	
FORESTER CAMP.- (28.N.9.a.9.5.)	13th		Composite Battalion moved in the evening to RIDGE WOOD CAMP	
RIDGE WOOD CAMP -	14th			
RIDGE WOOD CAMP -	15th		At 4 a.m. camp was heavily shelled by enemy and Battalion moved to surrounding fields. Casualties:- 16th S.F. 1 O.R. killed. 17th KRRC 2/Lt. GOURDIE,/1 O.R. killed, 6 O.R. wounded (wounded)	
			Battalion moved to SCOTTISH WOOD CAMP (28.H.35.b.)	

WAR DIARY
or
INTELLIGENCE SUMMARY.
(Erase heading not required.)

Army Form C. 2118.

Page 2.

Place	Date	Hour	Summary of Events and Information	Remarks and references to Appendices
	16th		SCOTTISH WOOD CAMP. - Two Companies Sherwood Foresters proceeded to the line WYTSCHAETE Ridge taking up position of front line trench in front of the Grand BOIS De WYTSCHAETE and at 7.45pm. were ordered to attack - objective being ridge 1,000 yards to our front - 7th Bn. Seaforth Highlanders were on our right. 800 yards were gained and number of machine guns and prisoners were captured. The two remaining companies(Rifles) were ordered to go to 28.M.4.d. near RENINGHELST. Casualties. 16th S.F. Major MILLER,DSO., Capt. WRIGHT, 2/Lieut.SMITH Wounded. 13 O.R. killed, 6 O.R. Died of Wounds, 74 wounded, 8 missing. 17th K.R.Rif.C. 1 O.R. Wounded.	
	Night 16/17th		On arrival of the two Rifle Companies at 28.M.4.d. they were ordered back to the trenches, immediately, in the WYTSCHAETE Sector. These Companies were put in support and remained there during the day 17th., the whole Battalion coming under the orders of the 9th Division. Casualties. 16th S.F. 2/Lieut. EDWARDS, wounded, 17th K.R.R.C. 3 O.R. killed. 6 wounded.	
	18th		"A" and "B" Companies(Sherwood Foresters) and Battalion Headquarters were relieved by South African Troops and proceeded to billets at SCOTTISH WOOD CAMP arriving at 2.30am. "C" and "D" Companies(Rifles) remained under orders of the 1st South African Regt. Casualties:- 16th S.F. 2 O.R. Wounded. 17th K.R.R.C. 12 O.R. killed, 27 O.R. wounded. 16th R.B. 10 O.R. killed, 14 wounded, 4 missing.	
	19th		SCOTTISH WOOD CAMP. - The Battalion evacuated Camp at midnight 19/20th owing to heavy enemy shelling, 12 casualties. Battalion Headquarters and two Companies(Sherwood Foresters) moved to dugouts in ENGLISH WOOD(28.H.29.d.) and afterwards to AWAFUNI LINES (28.H.23.c.3.7.) Two Sherwood Companies proceeded to the WYTSCHAETE Sector and relieved the two Rifle Companies who returned to AWAFUNI LINES.	

Army Form C. 2118.

WAR DIARY
or
INTELLIGENCE SUMMARY.
(Erase heading not required.)

Instructions regarding War Diaries and Intelligence Summaries are contained in F. S. Regs., Part II. and the Staff Manual respectively. Title pages will be prepared in manuscript.

Place	Date	Hour	Summary of Events and Information	Remarks and references to Appendices
			Page 3.	
	19th cont.		Casualties:- 16th S.F. Capt.CLAYTON wounded, 2/Lieut.MOORE killed, 10 O.R. wounded. 17th K.R.Rif.C. 12 O.R. wounded, 14 missing. 16th R.B. 1 O.R. wounded, 1 missing.	
AWAPUNI LINES	20th		Sherwood Companies relieved and proceeded to rejoin remainder of Battalion at camp. Casualties:- 16th S.F. 6 O.R. wounded.	
AWAPUNI LINES	21st-24th		Working Parties found daily. Casualties 23rd. 16th S.F. 1 O.R. killed.	
AWAPUNI LINES	25th		Enemy opened very heavy bombardment of forward and rear areas at 2.45am. (Gas shelling included) and Battalion was forced to evacuate camp and take up position in the surrounding fields with B.H.Q. at 28.H.17.c.3.5. Battalion remained thus until 9 a.m. Orders were then received for the Battalion under command of Captain G.V.TAYLOR,MC., to proceed to G.H.Q. Second Line running from RIDGE WOOD to KRUISSTRAATHOEK Crossroads, which was completed by 12 noon. Orders received to withdraw from G.H.Q. Second Line and form a defensive flank from VIERSTRAAT Crossroads to southern edge of DICKEBUSCH Lake. The enemy had broken through across the VIERSTRAAT Crossroads, ~~xxxxxxxxxxxxxxxxxxxxxxxxxx~~ so Company of 17th Bn. K.R.R.C. and 16th R.B. formed a line from southern edge of RIDGE WOOD to CONFUSION CORNER (28.N.10.b.8.4.) the Sherwood Company being echeloned behind them to southern point of Dickebusch Lake. Casualties:- 16th S.F. 1 O.R. died of wounds, 5 wounded. 17th K.R.R.C. 2 O.R. wounded. Captain J.DOBSON wounded. 16th R.B. 1 O.R. wounded.	
	26th		Orders were received to withdraw the Sherwood Company and send them to G.H.Q. First Line VOORMEZEELE, where they came under the orders of O.C. No.1 Composite Battalion. This was carried out without casualties. Two Companies of the 6th Leicestershire Regt. were sent up to reinforce No.3 Composite Battalion and dug in a line from 28 N.5.c.5.9. to 28.N.4.c.6.9. At 2 p.m. enemy was seen to be massing troops on left behind VIERSTRAAT Crossroads and Brasserie and the artillery were put on to them. Machine Gun and Rifle fire was opened and terrific casualties inflicted upon the enemy completely breaking up any counter-attack that was to be launched against our line. On the right we were in touch with the New Zealand Cyclist Corps and on left with 1st Bn.Lincolnshire Regt.	

WAR DIARY
or
INTELLIGENCE SUMMARY.
(Erase heading not required.)

Army Form C. 2118.

Page 4.

Place	Date	Hour	Summary of Events and Information	Remarks and references to Appendices
	26th	cont.	Casualties:- 16th S.F. 5 O.R. killed, 5 O.R. wounded, 21 missing. 17th K.R.Rif.C. Lieut. BUTCHART wounded, 18 O.R. wounded, 4 killed, 4 missing. 16th R.B. 5 O.R. killed, 4 wounded, 3 missing.	
	27th		At 1 a.m. the Rifle Company was relieved in the line by two Companies of 13/14th Northumberland Fusiliers and were ordered to proceed to take up position from KRUISTRAATHOEK Cross Roads to SCOTTISH WOOD in G.H.Q. Second Line. This Company was relieved by 19th King's Liverpool Regiment and the Sherwood Company under orders of No.1. Composite Battalion. The whole Battalion proceeded to camp at DOMINION LINES (near OUDERDOM 28.G.17.d.3.1.) Casualties:- 16th S.F. Lieut. A.H. STRUTT, died of wounds, 5 O.R. died of wounds. 26 wounded. 17th K.R.R.C. 4 O.R. wounded. 16th R.B. 1 O.R. wounded.	
	28/29th		DOMINION LINES.- Enemy shelled camp morning of 29th and Battalion vacated it occupying old trench line to the rear of the camp. Nos. 2 & 3 Composite Battalions amalgamated (consisting of 16th Sherwood Foresters, 17th King's Royal Rifle Corps, 16th Rifle Brigade, 11th Royal Sussex Regt., 13th Royal Sussex Regt., and 13th Gloucestershire Regt.) under the command of Lieut.-Colonel WILKINSON (Commanding Officer 1/1st Herts Regt.) Casualties:- 16th S.F. 12 O.R. wounded. 17th K.R.R.C. 8 O.R. wounded.	
	30th		G.17.d.1.3. in trench line in rear of DOMINION CAMP. Casualties:- 16th S.F. 1 O.R. wounded.	

(sd) G.V. TAYLOR, Captain & Adjutant.,
for Officer Commanding No.3 Battalion, 39th Divisional Composite Brigade.

APPENDIX "A".

Copy of letter received from 39th Divl. Comp. Bde.

Os.C. Nos.1,2,3 and 4 Bns., 118th T.M.Bty.

The following telegram from Second Army has been received:-

"The Army Commander wishes to place on record his appreciation of the gallant conduct of the troops under your command in the present fighting. It is worthy of all praise and he wishes all ranks to be informed"

(sd) F.H.MARR, Captain,
Brigade Major, 39th Composite Brigade.

APPENDIX "B".

Copy of letter received from 39th Div. Comp. Bde.

Os.C. Nos.1,2,3 & 4 Bns., T.M.Bty.

"The Corps Commander has expressed his great admiration at the manner in which all ranks of the 39th Composite Brigade have responded to the various calls made upon them.
The gallantry displayed by Nos.2 & 3 Bns. under most difficult conditions is deserving of special praise.
The Brigadier General Commanding desires to thank all ranks for the excellent way in which they have maintained the traditions of the 39th Division.

(sd) F.H.MARR, Captain,
Brigade Major, 39th Composite Brigade.

APPENDIX "C"

Copy of letter received from Major General Comanding, 21st Division.

39th Divisional Composite Brigade.
"Well done the 39th Division.
You have done splendid work under the most adverse circumstances and I am sure you will continue to do so whenever your services are required.
I fully realize what you have been through and cannot express my admiration for the behaviour of all ranks".

(sd) DAVID M.CAMPBELL, Major-General,
Commanding 21st Division.

H.Q., 21st Division.
28.4.18.

117th Brigade.

39th Division
Composite Brigade.

Formed part of No. 3 Composite Battalion 10.4.18.

1/16th BATTALION

NOTTS & DERBY REGIMENT

APRIL 1918.

11th Leinster Bat Pl.

Army Form C. 2118.

11/39

WAR DIARY
or
INTELLIGENCE SUMMARY.
(Erase heading not required.)

YA 26

Place	Date	Hour	Summary of Events and Information	Remarks and references to Appendices
	1918		"April"	
Longues	1st		11 Battalion proceeded in Motor Lorries from Longues to Boyelles.	MB.
Boyelles	2nd		Cleaning up and reorganisation.	MB.S.
	3rd		To Details and Stragglers reported.	MB.
			The Battalion proceeded by March Route from Boyelles to Metigny.	
Metigny	4th		The Battalion proceeded by March Route from Metigny to Forceville, and was inspected en route by Major General Blacklock C.M.G. D.S.O. Commanding 39th Division.	MB.S.
Forceville	5th		Rest	MB.
	6th		The Battalion proceeded by March Route to Frequires.	25A 9 General

Army Form C. 2118.

WAR DIARY
or
INTELLIGENCE SUMMARY.
(Erase heading not required.)

Instructions regarding War Diaries and Intelligence Summaries are contained in F. S. Regs., Part II, and the Staff Manual respectively. Title pages will be prepared in manuscript.

Place	Date	Hour	Summary of Events and Information	Remarks and references to Appendices
FLEQUIRES	7th		Rest	
	8th		A & D Companies proceeded by tram to ST OMER and acted as Brigade entraining party	
	9th		The remainder of the Battalion proceeded by tram to ST OMER, and then by March Route to MOULLE, where billets were taken over. B & C Companies following the same evening	
MOULLE	10th		The right of 10th, 11th and 1 OFFICERS 302 OTHER RANKS and Battalion transport moved to VLAMERTINGHE from ST OMER by Rail to form part of No. 3 Cambride Battalion 29th Division Cambride Brigade	
VSTERGAUZ	11th		Details of the Battalion proceeded by March Route from MOULLE to VSTERGAUZ. No. 3 Cambride Battalion proceeded by March Route from VLAMERTINGHE to ALBERTA CAMP.	

WAR DIARY
or
INTELLIGENCE SUMMARY.
(Erase heading not required.)

Army Form C. 2118.

Place	Date	Hour	Summary of Events and Information	Remarks and references to Appendices
LISTERGAUZ	12th		80 OTHER RANKS from Details proceeded with No.5 Composite Battalion for attachment to the 1/1st AUSTRALIAN DIVISION. No. 3 Composite Battalion (under the command of LIEUT. COL. the HON. E. COKE. D.S.O. M.C.) moved by light railway from TENECOTON to JEHLECOE SIDING and billeted in FORESTERS CAMP. The Battalion came under orders of the 21st DIVISION	
	13th		Battalion Details of 1 OFFICER and 30 OTHER RANKS proceeded from LISTERGAUZ to RECQUES. Casualties :- 1 OTHER RANK WOUNDED No. 3 Composite Battalion moved to RIDGE WOOD CAMP	
	14th		MAJOR J.S. GASSY M.C. assumed Command of the Battalion	
RIDGE WOOD CAMP.	15th		No 3 Composite Battalion at RIDGE WOOD CAMP heavily shelled by enemy at 4 am and moved to SCOTTISH WOOD CAMP Casualties :- 1 OTHER RANK KILLED 3 OTHER RANKS WOUNDED.	

WAR DIARY
or
INTELLIGENCE SUMMARY

Army Form C. 2118.

Place	Date	Hour	Summary of Events and Information	Remarks and references to Appendices
WYTSCHAETE	16th		A.B.B Companies (16th Battalion SHERWOOD FORESTERS) No.3 Combouvé Battalion under the Command of Major J.W.T. MILLAR DSO DCM proceeded to the line at WYTSCHAETE RIDGE taking up position at the front line trench in front of the GRAND BOIS de WYTSCHAETE, and at 11.45 am were ordered to attack objective being ridge 1000 yards to our front. The 7th Battalion SEAFORTH HIGHLANDERS were on our right. 800 yards were gained and a number of Machine Guns and Prisoners were captured Major J.W.T. MILLAR DSO DCM. Captain W.E. WRIGHT M.C and 2nd Lieut J.C. SMITH "WOUNDED" Casualties. 13 other ranks KILLED 6 DIED of WOUNDS. 74 WOUNDED and 8 MISSING.	N.B.
	17th		2nd Lieut W EDWARDS "WOUNDED"	N.B.
SCOTTISH WOOD CAMP	18th		A.B Companies (16th Battalion SHERWOOD FORESTERS) No3 Combouvé Battalion were relieved by South African Troops and proceeded to huts at SCOTTISH WOOD CAMP. Casualties - 2 other ranks "WOUNDED"	N.B.

WAR DIARY
or
INTELLIGENCE SUMMARY.
(Erase heading not required.)

Army Form C. 2118.

Place	Date	Hour	Summary of Events and Information	Remarks and references to Appendices
ENGLISH WOOD CAMP.	19th		The No.3 Cmbooli Battalion evacuated SCOTTISH WOOD CAMP at midnight owing to heavy Enemy Shelling and moved to Dug-Outs in ENGLISH WOOD. A.W.B. Companies (16th Battalion SHERWOOD FORESTERS) proceeded to WYTSCHAETE SECTOR and relieved the two RIFLE Companies of the No.3 Cmbooli Battalion. Casualties:- 2nd Lieut C.A.G. MOORE. KILLED. Captain C. CLAYTON WOUNDED. 10 OTHER RANKS WOUNDED.	
AWAPUNI CAMP.	20th		A.W.B. Companies No.3 Cmbooli Battalion relieved and proceeded to CAMP. AWAPUNI. Casualties:- 6. OTHER RANKS WOUNDED. LINES	
	23rd		Casualties:- 1. OTHER RANK KILLED.	
	25th		The No.3 Cmbooli Battalion) Enemy opened very heavy bombardment of forward and rear areas at 2.45 am and Battalion was forced to evacuate Camp	

Army Form C. 2118.

WAR DIARY
or
INTELLIGENCE SUMMARY.
(Erase heading not required.)

Instructions regarding War Diaries and Intelligence Summaries are contained in F.S. Regs., Part II. and the Staff Manual respectively. Title pages will be prepared in manuscript.

Place	Date	Hour	Summary of Events and Information	Remarks and references to Appendices
VIERSTRAAT.	25th	—	Orders were received to proceed to G.H.Q. 2nd line running from RIDGE WOOD to KRUISSTRAATHOEK Cross Roads which was Completed by 12 noon. The enemy had broken through across the VIERSTRAAT Cross Roads. On orders being received to withdraw and form a defensive flank from VIERSTRAAT Cross Roads to Southern edge of DICKIE BUSCH LAKE. The Company of the 16th Battalion SHERWOOD FORESTERS was echeloned behind the 17th Battalion R.R.R Corps and 16th Battalion RIFLE BRIGADE Companies. Casualties. — 1 OTHER RANK "DIED OF WOUNDS" 5 OTHER RANKS "WOUNDED"	W.B
VOORMEZEELE.	26th	—	(On the No 3 Composite Battalion) Orders were received to withdraw the 16th Battalion SHERWOOD FORESTERS Company and send them to G.H.Q. line VOORMEZEELE where they came under orders of the No.1 Composite Battalion. Casualties :- 5 OTHER RANKS KILLED. 5 OTHER RANKS WOUNDED 21 OTHER RANKS "MISSING"	No 2
DOMINION CAMP.	27th	—	The No 3 Composite Battalion relieved and proceeded to DOMINION CAMP.	

WAR DIARY
or
INTELLIGENCE SUMMARY.

(Erase heading not required.)

Army Form C. 2118.

Place	Date	Hour	Summary of Events and Information	Remarks and references to Appendices
Dominion Camp	27th		2 Officers and 9 Other Ranks attached to No1. Battalion 307th Infantry Regiment A.E.F. as Instructors.	N.K.R.
			Casualties:- Lieut. A.H. Strutt "Wounded" 5 Other Ranks "Died of Wounds" 26 Other Ranks "Wounded"	
	28th		1 Officer and 9 Other Ranks attached to No.3. Battalion 307th Infantry Regiment A.E.F. as Instructors.	N.K.R.
	"		No. 2 & 3 Composite Battalions amalgamated under the command of Lieut. Col. Wilkinson (Commanding officer of 11/1st Herts Regiment.)	
	29th		Enemy shelled Dominion Camp and the Battalion proceeded to trenches old German line to the rear of the Camp	N.K.R.
			Casualties:- 12 Other Ranks "Wounded"	
	30th		Casualties:- 1 Other Rank "Wounded"	

[signature] Lieut Col
Commanding 16th Battalion [illegible]

WAR DIARY
or
INTELLIGENCE SUMMARY.

(Erase heading not required.)

Army Form C. 2118.

Place	Date	Hour	Summary of Events and Information	Remarks and references to Appendices

APPENDIX "A"

Copy of letter received from 39th Divisional Composite Brigade to Nos. 1, 2, 3 & 4th Battalions, 118th Trench Mortar Battery.

The following telegram from Second Army has been received:-

"The Army Commander wishes to place on record his appreciation of the gallant conduct of the troops under your Command in the present fighting. It is worthy of all praise and he wishes all ranks to be informed."

Sd. G. H. Mare   Captain
Brigade Major, 39th Composite Brigade.

APPENDIX "B"

Copy of letter received from 39th Divisional Composite Brigade to Nos. 1, 2, 3 & 4th Battalions, Trench Mortar Battery.

Army Form C. 2118.

WAR DIARY
or
INTELLIGENCE SUMMARY.
(Erase heading not required.)

Place	Date	Hour	Summary of Events and Information	Remarks and references to Appendices
			APPENDIX "B" Continued.	
			The Corps Commander has expressed his great admiration at the manner in which all ranks of the 39th Composite Brigade have responded to the various calls made upon them. The gallantry displayed by Nos. 2 & 3 Battalions under most difficult conditions is deserving of special praise. The Brigadier General Commanding desires to thank all ranks for the excellent way in which they have maintained the traditions of the 39th Division. Sd. I H Mars Captain Brigade Major 39th Composite Brigade	
			APPENDIX "C"	
			Copy of letter received from Major General Commanding 21st Division. 39th Divisional Composite Brigade	

Army Form C. 2118.

WAR DIARY
or
INTELLIGENCE SUMMARY.
(Erase heading not required.)

APPENDIX "C" Continued

Well done the 39th Division.

You have done splendid work under the most adverse circumstances and I am sure you will continue to do so wherever your services are required. I fully realise what you have been through and cannot express my admiration for the behaviour of all ranks.

Sd. David M. Campbell
Major General
Commanding 21st Division

A.Q. 21st Division
28.4.18